Explore!
RAINFOREST

Jen Green

WAYLAND

Printed in 2015

Dewey Number: 333.7'5-dc23
ISBN 978 0 7502 8380 9

Wayland, an imprint of
Hachette Children's Group
Part of Hodder & Stoughton
Carmelite House
50 Victoria Embankment
London EC4Y 0DZ

Editors: Vicky Brooker and Julia Adams
Designer: Elaine Wilkinson
Picture Researcher: Shelley Noronha
Illustrations for step-by-steps: Peter Bull

10 9 8 7 6 5 4 3 2

First published in 2014 by Wayland
Copyright © Wayland 2014

Printed in Malaysia

An Hachette UK Company

www.hachette.co.uk

www.hachettechildrens.co.uk

Picture acknowledgements:
The author and publisher would like to thank the following agencies and people for allowing these pictures to be reproduced:

p. 1 (LH image) & p. 15: Robin Tenison/Getty Images; p. 3 & 16/17: Naturepl.com; p. 5 (bottom): Michael & Patricia Fogden/Corbis; p. 13 (bottom): Frans Lanting Studio/Alamy; p. 14: NHPA/Photoshot; pp. 14/15: Herve Collart/Sygma/Corbis; p. 17 (top): British Library Board/Robana/TopFoto; p. 17 (bottom): Topham Picturepoint/TopFoto; p. 18 (rosy periwinkle image): Edward Parker/ Alamy; p. 18 (calabar beans image): Science Photo Library/Alamy; p. 22: LatinContent/Getty Images; p. 23 (top): Cyril Ruso/Minden Pictures/FLPA; p. 23 (bottom): NHPA/Photoshot; p. 25 (top): Greg Vaughn/ Getty Images; p. 25 (bottom): Woodfall Wild Images/Photoshot; p. 26: Peter Oxford/Getty Images;
All other images and creative graphics: Shutterstock

Please note:
The website addresses (URLs) included in this book were valid at the time of going to press. However, because of the nature of the Internet, it is possible that some addresses may have changed, or sites may have changed or closed down since publication. While the author and publishers regret any inconvenience this may cause to the readers, no responsibility for any such changes can be accepted by either the author or the publishers.

Contents

Where in the World?

Tropical rainforests are very special places.
Mighty trees soar upwards, forming a green, leafy roof.
The air is hot and sticky. These ancient forests cover just
a small fraction of the Earth's surface, but are home to an
amazing 50-70 per cent of all living things found on land.

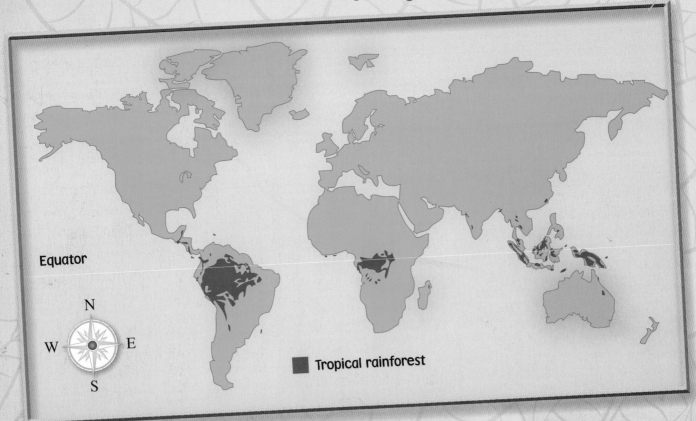

Equator

N
W E
S

■ Tropical rainforest

Tropical rainforests form a green belt around the Equator. The largest
forests are in South and Central America, West Africa and Southeast Asia.
Rainforests also grow in southern Asia and northeastern Australia.

Location

Tropical rainforests lie in a narrow band ten degrees north and south of the Equator. The tropical Sun beats down fiercely, so rainforests are hot all year round. Daytime temperatures hover around 25°C, with little variation between the seasons. Most tropical rainforests are low-lying. Conditions are a little cooler in upland forests, which are called cloud forests because they are often covered in mist and cloud. The Amazon Rainforest in South America is the world's largest rainforest.

Rivers and streams run through rainforests, draining water from the land.

Rainfall

Rainforests lie in the path of moist winds blowing off tropical oceans. Skies are often clear at dawn, but by midday, clouds form from moisture that has evaporated in the hot sunlight. Rain falls during most afternoons. Tropical rainforests receive over 200 cm of rainfall a year – nearly three times the rainfall of London.

Shy, piglike tapirs live in the rainforests of South America and Southeast Asia.

Variety

These forests contain far more species than any other habitat on land. This variety is called biodiversity. Just one hectare of rainforest may contain 200 different types of trees – that's 20 times the number that grow in a similar-sized patch of woodland in Europe or North America. What's more, each tree may support dozens of different plants, and hundreds of different animals, large and small.

Forest layers

Scientists studying life in rainforests divide the forest into vertical layers called storeys. Trees rooted in the ground shoot upwards in a layer called the understorey. Some 40 m above the ground, trees spread their branches and twigs to form a leafy layer called the canopy. Tall trees called emergents rise above the canopy to form the topmost layer. The tallest forest trees grow to 70 m tall.

Canopy

The canopy forms a dense mesh of leaves about 10 m thick. This layer absorbs almost all of the light and moisture that bathes the forest. The leaves, buds, flowers and fruits of the canopy provide food for flying creatures such as birds, bats and insects, and for nimble climbers such as monkeys.

Toucans live in South America. The long beak allows it to reach fruit growing on slender twigs.

Understorey

The canopy shades most of the light and moisture from the layer below, called the understorey. The vegetation here includes palm trees, shrubs and young trees – and the huge, straight trunks of large forest trees. Vines and trailing lianas form rope-like walkways for animals climbing up to feed in the canopy, or dropping down to the ground. Most food is in the layer above, so there is less reason for animals to linger here.

This vine has wrapped itself around a tree and coiled upwards towards the light.

Forest floor

Only a tiny fraction of the light and moisture in a rainforest filters through to ground level. This makes the forest floor dry and shady. Vegetation is fairly sparse, except along rivers and in sunny clearings where a mighty forest tree has fallen. The thick carpet of leaves hides small creatures such as millipedes and prowling predators such as snakes and spiders.

Snakes such as this false coral snake lurk among the moss and dead leaves on the forest floor.

Rainforest glider

Some animals that live high in the canopy are known as fliers. 'Flying lemurs' cannot really fly. But they glide between trees using flaps of skin stretched between their limbs and tail. When the animal launches into the air, these flaps act like a parachute, slowing the animal's fall.

Flying lemurs, also called colugos, live in the rainforests of Southeast Asia.

You will need:

A piece of paper (A4-size)

Scissors

Sticky tape

Pencil and coloured pens

1 Fold over a 2 cm wide strip at the top end of the paper. Fold this strip over three more times, making sure you press each fold down firmly.

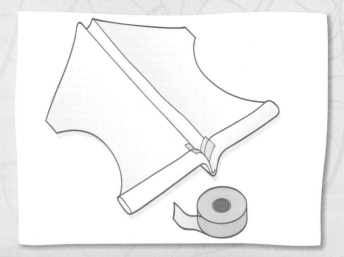

2 Fold the paper in half lengthways, with the previous folds facing inwards. With your pencil, mark up the shape of a lemur's body (as shown) and cut it out.

3 Make two additional folds lengthways, 1 cm either side of the central fold, to form a keel shape. Use sticky tape to fasten the keel at the front.

4 Make 1 cm folds in the lemur's feet, so the front paws fold upwards, and the back paws fold downwards.

5 Use felt-tip pens or coloured pencils to draw the lemur's face and colour the body.

Fly your glider!

Hold your glider along the central keel and launch it into the air.
Adjust the flaps to alter the flight path.

Feeding and food chains

The relationships between living things in a rainforest can be shown in food chains. Many food chains build up to form a food web like the one opposite. The connections between living things mean that if one species fails to thrive in the forest, it affects the creatures above and below it in the food chain.

Plants

Plants form the base of rainforest food chains. They use photosynthesis to make their own food and produce leafy growth. Plant foods such as leaves, sap, fruits, nuts, pollen and nectar provide fuel for animals. Some animals help plants by spreading their seeds.

Hummingbirds sip flower nectar using their long, delicate beaks.

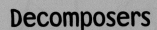

Decomposers

When rainforest plants and animals die, their remains are broken down by decomposers such as insects, fungi and microscopic bacteria. This returns minerals to the soil where they nourish plants, forming the last links in the food web. Rainforest soil is low in nutrients because the minerals are quickly absorbed by plants. The warm, wet conditions in rainforests speed the rotting process.

Fungi absorb nutrients from dead plants and animals.

Jaguar

Agouti

Tapir

Plants and flowers

Predators and prey

All animals depend on plants for food either directly or indirectly. Herbivores (plant-eaters) such as sloths, bats and hummingbirds feed on plant foods such as leaves, pollen and nectar. In turn, plant-eaters provide food for carnivorous (meat-eating) predators large and small, from hawks and jaguars to snakes and centipedes.

Other rainforest animals such as baboons and wild boar eat both plant and animal foods.

This picture shows part of a food web in the Amazon rainforest.

Why are rainforests important?

Rainforests take up only a small fraction of the Earth's land area, but are important to the whole planet. As well as being vital for wildlife, they influence the Earth's climate and help to maintain a healthy balance of gases in the atmosphere.

Adding oxygen

During photosynthesis, forest trees and plants absorb carbon dioxide and give out oxygen, which animals and people need to breathe. Rainforest trees lock up carbon dioxide, but when forests are cut down and burned, carbon dioxide is released. Carbon dioxide is a greenhouse gas – in the atmosphere, it traps the Sun's heat, acting like the glass in a greenhouse. This increases temperatures worldwide, producing global warming.

Scientists believe the Earth's largest rainforest, the Amazon, produces a fifth of the world's oxygen.

Water cycle

Rainforests increase rainfall in the surrounding region. This is because the forests act like sponges. When it rains, trees and plants soak up water and later release it slowly. Moisture evaporates from leaves and gathers in the air to form clouds which bring more rain. In this way, rainforests recycle moisture that would otherwise drain away into the oceans. If the forests are cut down, it can lead to drought.

Dark clouds form from moisture evaporated from a rainforest.

Erosion

The roots of rainforest trees and plants anchor the soil, helping to prevent erosion. If forests are cut down, the soil washes away after heavy rain. This can cause landslides and floods as well as the loss of valuable forest soil.

Erosion is common on rainforest land that has been logged.

Rainforest people

Rainforests worldwide are home to hundreds of different peoples, such as the Kayapo of the Amazon and the Baka of Africa. These groups have a deep understanding of their surroundings. Over the centuries, they have learned how to harvest the forest's resources sustainably, without upsetting the delicate balance of nature.

Baka tribesman hunting with a crossbow.

Wild food

Rainforest peoples traditionally live by hunting and gathering wild foods such as roots, fruits, nuts and honey. Groups such as the Yanomami of the Amazon hunt with arrows and blowpipe darts dipped in poison from deadly plants or the skin of poisonous frogs. Rainforests traditionally have small populations, with only a few people hunting and gathering wild food from a large area.

Farming

Many forest peoples clear small patches of rainforest to grow crops such as yam, maize, beans or sweet potatoes. Healing plants are also grown (rainforest peoples know hundreds of plant medicines). These small plots are known as gardens. After a few years, the thin forest soil becomes unproductive. The group moves on and clears a new patch of forest. They return to harvest fruits and medicines from the old plot, which becomes overgrown and eventually returns to the forest. This traditional form of farming has little impact on the rainforest.

An Amazonian Indian digs in a garden plot using a traditional digging stick.

Living by water

Many rainforest groups live by rivers and lakes which provide food, water and also a means of transport. Travel by canoe is the only way of moving through dense forest quickly and easily. Dugout canoes are carved from a single tree trunk. Their thick base prevents tipping. Houses by rivers are often built on stilts to guard against flooding. Houses are built of local materials such as bamboo, and thatched with large, waxy leaves or grasses.

This small village has been built in a clearing by the Amazon River in Brazil.

New arrivals

Since the 1500s, increasing numbers of outsiders have settled in rainforests. The newcomers move in to farm or to work in industries such as logging, mining or ranching. Some settlements that were once tiny villages have grown into sprawling towns and cities, which eat into the forest.

Discovery

In 1492, Italian explorer Christopher Columbus became one of the first Europeans to set eyes on a tropical rainforest. He wrote: "I never beheld so fair a thing; trees beautiful and green and different from ours, with flowers and fruits each according to their kind...". Later, scientists identified thousands of unknown plant and animal species, and marvelled at the variety of rainforest life. Hundreds of new species are still discovered every year.

These forest people are of mixed European and Amazonian Indian descent.

Sugar plantations and mills were worked by slaves brought from Africa, who were badly treated.

Exploitation

More Europeans arrived after explorers such as Columbus. They soon claimed huge expanses of forest for their own countries. They harvested resources such as timber and minerals. They set up plantations to grow crops such as rubber and sugar cane. Many local people died of diseases brought by Europeans.

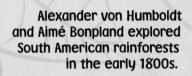

Alexander von Humboldt and Aimé Bonpland explored South American rainforests in the early 1800s.

New settlers

In the twentieth and twenty-first century, settlement of the rainforests has continued. In the last 50 years or so, the governments of rainforest countries such as Brazil and Indonesia have encouraged city people to move to rainforests to escape poverty and overcrowding in cities. The newcomers cut down more forest to farm crops, increasing pressure on the forest and its original inhabitants.

Rainforest produce

Tropical rainforests may be far away, but we use all sorts of forest resources in our daily lives. Rainforest products include timber, rubber, bamboo and minerals. Foods such as dates, bananas and cocoa originally grew wild in one rainforest region. Now, they are grown in plantations all over the Tropics. Many medicines are made from rainforest plants.

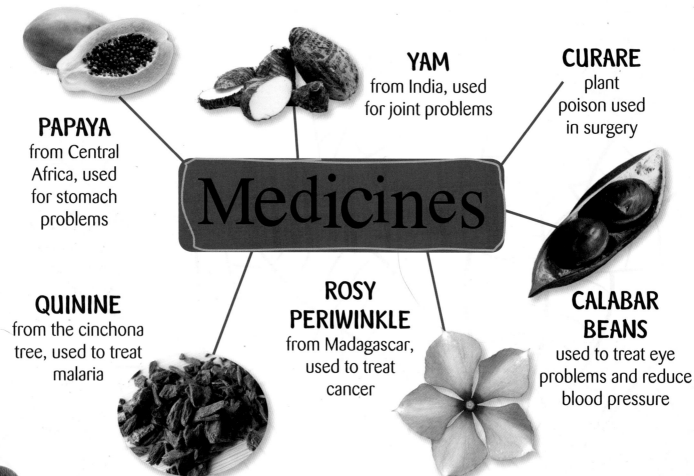

YAM
from India, used
for joint problems

CURARE
plant
poison used
in surgery

PAPAYA
from Central
Africa, used
for stomach
problems

Medicines

QUININE
from the cinchona
tree, used to treat
malaria

**ROSY
PERIWINKLE**
from Madagascar,
used to treat
cancer

**CALABAR
BEANS**
used to treat eye
problems and reduce
blood pressure

FRUITS
avocados, bananas, pineapples, lemons, papaya, starfruit and breadfruit

SPICES
nutmeg, cinnamon, cloves, ginger, pepper and vanilla (used to flavour foods)

CHICLE
sap used to make chewing gum

Foods

COFFEE BEANS
used to make coffee

NUTS
peanuts, cashew nuts, Brazil nuts and macadamia nuts

SUGAR
from sugar cane, a tropical grass

OIL
from oil palms used in cooking, soap and cosmetics

VEGETABLES
manioc, sweet potatoes, yams and cassava

COCOA
beans used to make chocolate

RUBBER
made from a tree sap called latex

BAMBOO
used to make furniture and garden canes

HARDWOOD TIMBER
used to make furniture, floors and fittings

Materials

19

Rainforest recipe

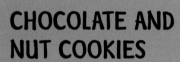

Rainforest ingredients such as chocolate, nuts and sugar can be used to make all sorts of delicious recipes. These rainforest cookies will make a tasty treat in your lunchbox or a snack between meals.

CHOCOLATE AND NUT COOKIES

You will need:

330g flour

1 tsp bicarbonate of soda

1 tsp salt

225g butter or margarine, softened

150g caster sugar

150g soft brown sugar

1 tsp vanilla extract

2 large eggs

330g chocolate chips or dark chocolate, crumbled

1 cup of peanuts or macadamia nuts, coarsely chopped

1 Set the oven to 190°C (170°C if it is fan-assisted). Mix the flour, baking soda and salt in a small bowl.

2 In a second bowl, mix the butter, sugar and vanilla extract until creamy.

Add the eggs to the butter mixture one at a time, and mix in well.

3 Gradually add the flour mixture and stir in well. Add the chocolate and nuts and mix well.

4 Divide the mixture in two. Roll into two long sausage shapes and then cut into slices. Lay on a greased baking tray.

5 Bake in the preheated oven for about ten minutes until golden-brown. Allow the cookies to cool before serving.

Paradise lost

Sadly, the world's rainforests are under threat. A mere two hundred years ago, these tropical forests covered about twice the area they do today. In the last 30 years, the pace of destruction has got faster. But what is causing these changes?

Logging and development

Logging is one of the main causes of deforestation, or forest destruction. Rainforests worldwide are being chopped down for their valuable hardwood timber, which is mainly shipped abroad to make furniture and decking. The wood is also used for fuel and to make paper. Forest land is bulldozed to make way for mines, roads and new towns to house people who have arrived from the cities. Large dams have been built on rivers to supply electricity to towns.

A giant rainforest tree is cut down in Cameroon.

Farming and ranching

Large expanses of forest have been cleared and burned to make way for farms and plantations where crops such as coffee, soya beans and oil palms are grown. Land is also cleared to ranch cattle. Most of the meat is shipped abroad to make hamburgers for sale in countries such as Britain. After a few years, the forest soil becomes infertile, so farmers and ranchers move on to clear a new path of forest.

Cattle graze on deforested land in the Amazon. Expanding cattle ranches are causing a lot of forests destruction.

This hardwood timber from the West African rainforest will be shipped and sold abroad.

Impact

When rainforests are cut down, animals from apes to ants lose their habitat. Scientists believe thousands of rainforest species are in danger of extinction, including many creatures that haven't even been identified. Forest peoples lose their homes, land and their way of life. As we have seen, rainforest destruction also affects local weather patterns and changes the balance of gases in the atmosphere. It can lead to erosion, floods and drought.

23

Rainforest conservation

Rainforest groups, conservation organisations, landowners and governments can all play a part in conservation. But saving the forests isn't easy. Countries where rainforests grow are mostly poor. Their governments say they need to harvest resources such as timber and minerals to make money and improve people's lives.

Managing resources

Rainforests can be managed sustainably. This means managing the forest carefully so resources can be harvested without damaging nature. Products such as rubber, palm fruits and Brazil nuts can be harvested without cutting down trees. Sustainable forestry means cutting down only a few trees and planting young trees to replace them.

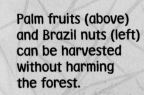

Palm fruits (above) and Brazil nuts (left) can be harvested without harming the forest.

Protected areas

Setting up national parks and reserves is one way to save whole rainforests and their wildlife. Since 2000, several large national parks have been set up in the Amazon. Logging and mining are carefully controlled. Tourists visiting the park bring in money which can be used for conservation or to pay local guides.

Elephants surround a tourist lodge in Thailand.

What can we do?

Rainforests grow in distant places, but their destruction affects the whole planet. Luckily, there are things we can all do to help protect these amazing forests. If your family buys hardwood furniture or decking, make sure the wood comes from a sustainable supplier. Join a conservation organisation that is working to save the rainforest. Organise a sponsored walk, swim or cycle to raise money for your favourite rainforest animal.

A worker plants tree seedlings in a rainforest in Southeast Asia.

25

Interview with a campaigner

Mongabay.com is an environmental website devoted to rainforest conservation. It was started in 1999 by American campaigner Rhett A. Butler. On the website, Rhett explains how he got involved and why it's important to save tropical forests.

A scientist studies life high in the canopy using a rope and sling.

Q How did Mongabay get started?

A The seeds for Mongabay.com were sown by a personal experience on the island of Borneo, when a beautiful tract of lowland forest was converted into wood chips for a paper pulp mill… I wanted to share the experience with those who hadn't witnessed the magnificence of these places. While they may be hot, bug-ridden, and remote, these forests have a lot to offer.

Q Why are rainforests being destroyed?

A Rainforests are being destroyed for many reasons, the greatest of which is economic. Poor people living in and around forests rely on rainforests for agriculture, fuelwood collection, bush meat and more. Families need to put food on the table. Industry relies on forests to supply raw materials for production and cheap land.

Q How do you feel about the destruction of rainforests and loss of biodiversity?

A I am deeply saddened and frustrated by the destruction of the rainforests. It's like smashing an ancient Roman vase solely to get a penny from inside – a tremendous waste of resources and natural beauty that is irreplaceable within our lifetime.

Q What can the public do to help save the rainforest?

A Avoid products derived from forests in an unsustainable way – like certain wood products. Become aware of issues that affect rainforests and tell your friends and parents why rainforests are important. Be environmentally responsible – recycle; do not waste water or electricity. Support rainforest conservation organisations and companies that offer sustainable rainforest products.

Read the full interview with Rhett on
www.mongabay.com/interview.htm
Find out more about Mongabay on kids.mongabay.com

Facts and figures

Percentage of rainforest on each continent:

Australia 9%

Southeast Asia 16%

Central and South America 45%

Africa 30%

Largest rainforest

The Amazon is the world's largest rainforest, covering 5,500,000 square kilometres – an area the size of the United States without Alaska. Sixty per cent of the forest lies in Brazil, with 13 per cent in Peru, 10 per cent in Colombia and small amounts in other countries.

Biodiversity

The Amazon rainforest contains more plant and animal species than any other habitat on land. About 12 per cent of all bird species, 10 per cent of all fish, 10 per cent of mammals and 8 per cent of amphibians are found in this vast forest.

Deforestation

Experts estimate that around 170,000 square kilometres of tropical forest are felled each year worldwide, which is an area the size of 2,400 football pitches every hour. Malaysian forests are disappearing very quickly – 140,000 hectares have been cut down each year since 2000.

Extinction

Some scientists estimate that as many as 50,000 species are being lost every year due to rainforest deforestation. That is 137 species every day.

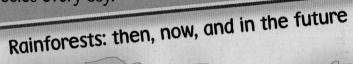

Rainforests: then, now, and in the future

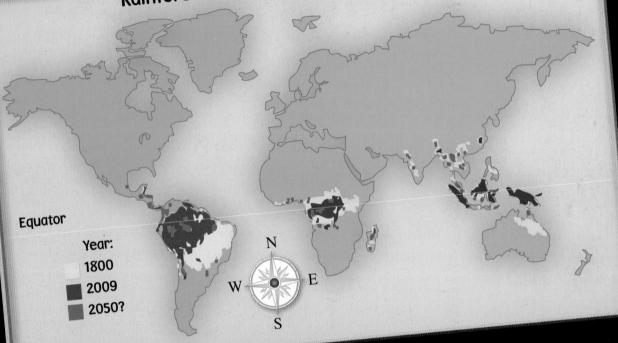

Equator

Year:
- 1800
- 2009
- 2050?

N
W E
S

The world's rainforests are disappearing fast. In 1800, they covered about 12 per cent of the Earth's land surface. Now, it is just 6 per cent. Almost all the rainforest could be gone by 2050 if destruction continues at the present rate.

Orang utans from Southeast Asian forests are now very scarce.

Conservation

Brazil contains some of the world's largest rainforest reserves. Jaú National Park in northwestern Brazil is an enormous protected area totalling 23,000 square kilometres. Tumucumaque National Park in the north is the same size as Belgium, covering about 3.8 million hectares.

Glossary

Biodiversity The variety of life in a particular habitat.

Canopy The dense, leafy layer found high above the ground in rainforests, formed by the interlocking branches of trees.

Carbon dioxide A gas absorbed by plants and given off by animals as they breathe.

Carnivorous Of animals that eat meat.

Conservation Work done to protect the natural world.

Decomposers Living things such as fungi, bacteria and beetles, which feed on dead plants and animals, and so speed up the rotting process.

Deforestation The cutting down and clearing of the rainforest.

Drought A long period without rain.

Emergent A tall tree which sticks up above the canopy in a rainforest.

Equator An imaginary line running around the middle of the Earth, at the widest point.

Global warming Rising temperatures around the world, caused by the build-up of greenhouse gases in the atmosphere.

Greenhouse gas One of a group of gases in the atmosphere that trap the Sun's heat near the planet surface. Carbon dioxide is a greenhouse gas.

Habitat A place where particular types of plants and animals live, such as a rainforest or desert.

Irreplaceable Something that cannot be replaced.

Lemur One of a group of primates found only on the African island of Madagascar, in rainforests and other habitats.

Oxygen A gas produced by plants, and which animals need to breathe.

Photosynthesis The process by which plants live and grow using sunlight energy, minerals and water from the soil.

Predator An animal that hunts other animals for food.

Prey An animal that is hunted by another.

Species A particular type of plant or animal, such as the orang utan, whose scientific name is *Pongo pygmaeus*.

Storeys The vertical layers of life in a rainforest, from the tallest trees down to the ground.

Sustainability Harvesting natural resources in a carefully managed way, so that nature is not harmed and the resources are preserved for the future.

Sustainable forestry A type of forestry that involves harvesting some timber without harming the forest.

Tract A large area.

Tropics The regions found on either side of the Equator, where the climate is hot all year round.

Understorey The layer below the canopy in a rainforest.

Further reading

BOOKS

Habitats and Wildlife in Danger by Sarah Levete, Wayland (2012)

Caring for Habitats by Jen Green, Wayland (2012)

Journey Along a River: The Amazon by Jen Green, Wayland (2012)

Maps of the Environmental World: Conservation Areas by Jack and Meg Gillett, Wayland (2011)

Travelling Wild: Trekking in the Congo Rainforest by Alex Woolf, Wayland (2013)

Websites

Mongabay: mongabay.com

Mongabay information about rainforests: kids.mongabay.com

Rainforest Action Network: ran.org and rainforestheroes.com

Rainforest Conservation Fund: www.rainforestconservation.org

Rainforest Alliance: www.rainforest-alliance.org/kids

Youth Earth Links: Rainforest Information Centre: www.rainforestinfo.org.au/children/chlinks.htm

Index